Why I Write in Coffee Houses and Diners

Why I Write in Coffee Houses and Diners

Selected Poems

Albert Huffstickler

Authors Choice Press
San Jose New York Lincoln Shanghai

Why I Write in Coffee Houses and Diners
Selected Poems

All Rights Reserved © 2000 by Albert Huffstickler

No part of this book may be reproduced or transmitted in any form or by any means, graphic, electronic, or mechanical, including photocopying, recording, taping, or by any information storage or retrieval system, without the permission in writing from the publisher.

Authors Choice Press
an imprint of iUniverse.com, Inc.

For information address:
iUniverse.com, Inc.
5220 S 16th, Ste. 200
Lincoln, NE 68512
www.iuniverse.com

Edited with an Introduction by Felicia Mitchell

Foreword by Chuck Taylor

Front Cover Photograph by John Vachon: Short Order Cafe, Moorhead, Iowa
Library of Congress, Prints & Photographs Division, FSA-OWI Collection, LC-USF33-T01-001731-M4 DLC

Back Cover Photograph by Dennis Cole:
Huffstickler Reading at La Dolce Vita, Austin, Texas, 1999

ISBN: 0-595-14014-9

Printed in the United States of America

Acknowledgments

Chapbooks and books where poems have appeared include *The Certitude of Laundromats* (Jamming Staplers Press, 1995), *Emergency Room* (SRLR Press, 1995), *Hindsight, or How I Survived the Depression* (Liquid Paper Press, 1997), *The Remembered Light* (Slough Press, 1980), *Soul Gallery* (Bard Press, 1987), *Working on My Death Chant* (Backyard Press, 1991), and *The Wander Years* (SRLR Press, 1998). Press of Circumstance Chapbooks in which poems have been printed include *Alienation, or the Billy the Kid Syndrome, Armageddon, Cafe du Jour, City of the Rain, The Cosmology of Madness, Fanfare for Lost Angels, Gleanings, Image in Brown, It's Lonely at the Bottom Too, Last-Minute Alterations, The Lost Poem, Notes of a Survivor, On the Doorstep of the Heart, People and More People, Quinlen, The Ruta Maya Poems, St. Francis Was a Flower Child,* and *The True Believer*. The author also gratefully acknowledges prior publication in the following journals: *Aileron, Anemone, American Jones, Artesian, The Atlanta Review, Atom Mind, Cerberus, Clark Street Review, Coffee House Poets' Quarterly, The Colorado-North Review, Concho River Review, Driver's Side Airbag, Fat Free, Fennel Stalk, First Class, Giants Play Well in the Drizzle, Green's Magazine, Ipsissima Verba, Lactuca, Lilliput Review, Main Street Rag, The New Writer, One Trick Pony, Patchwork Poems, Pecan Press, The Plastic Tower, Poetry Motel, Rattle, Slipstream, Tangents, The Texas Observer, Waterways: Poetry in the Mainstream,* and *Wayside Poetry Forum*.

To the Staff of General Libraries
The University of Texas at Austin
1974-1991

Contents

Foreword xi
Introduction xiii
The Way of Art 1
Condition 2
Meditation in Wyatt's 3
Coffee House Poets 4
Déjà Vu 5
The Visitation 6
Doppleganger 7
Rainbow Grill, Downtown Austin 8
Parameters 9
Father and Daughter 11
Mother and Daughter 12
Trial by Fire 13
A Ritual Song of Parting 14
At the Cafe Du Jour 15
Entrapment 17
Quandary 18
What You Will, or Love Among the Chicken Soup 19
Secrecy 20
Beliefs on Which We Stake Our Lives 21
Silent Night in Hyde Park 22
Old Acquaintance 23
The Plaza, Santa Fe 24
One of Those Times When Words Are Not Enough 25

Why I Write in Coffee Houses and Diners

The Way Things Come and Go	26
Report to Renee	27
Arby's Brenda	29
I Dreamed I Lived in Austin	31
Nostrum	34
Sanctuary	35
Christmas Lights	36
Grill Smoke	37
An End to Mourning	38
Ranch House Restaurant, Burnet, Texas	39
Claude	40
What It Means to Be Free	41
Quinlen's Promise	43
Bus at Night	44
Looking at the Ground	45
Wayfarer	47
Blood and Roses	48
Starburn	49
Madman on the Corner	50
Waiting for Sylvia	51
Coffee	53
The Lost Diner	54
At Wyatt's Cafeteria	56
The Plaza Cafe, Santa Fe	57
I Have a Dream	58
To My Twin Born Dead	59
Heart Song	60
Effort	61
Awaiting Clearance	62
Puzzle	63
October 31, 1981	64
Holidays, Holy Days	66

Albert Huffstickler

Thanksgiving 1985	67
Shelter	68
Saturday Morning, Cafe Du Jour	70
Oracle	71
Not Wounded, Sire, But Dead	72
Mandate from the Hag	73
A Requiem for Mad Helen	74
Cafe Du Jour	76
Cafe Poem	77
The Search	78
Vigil	79
Augury	80
Respite	81
Need	82
The Lost Poem	84
The Healing	86
Ministry	87
Echoes	88
Dream Come True	89
Key West	90
Markings	91
Queen of the Royal Castle	93
Found	94
Criminal Intent	95
A Blessing Poem	96
About the Author	99

Foreword

Recently I was sitting with Albert Huffstickler at the La Dolce Vita coffee shop in Hyde Park, Austin, when a small bus stopped at a corner and a class of students got out. They stood on the corner while a professor in a funny hat lectured and pointed up and down Duval Street.

The professor leads his class over to where we are sitting outside on the patio. "This is Albert Huffstickler," he says. "My hero."

"Yeah, I have this image," Albert observes dryly as the professor walks off with his class. "I don't do anything to maintain it, but if it helps reach an audience I let them think what they want."

I published Huffstickler's first book of poetry in 1979 on my small press, Slough Press, which has been dormant now for a number of years. The press has received over the years plenty of grants from the Texas Arts Commission and won many awards. Some of its authors went on to be famous, like Marion Winik, but I have never been prouder of any book than the one we did first when I and my family were "back-to-the-land hippies" in northeast Texas. In those days printing and publishing books was cheap. I think I got five hundred copies of *The Reflected Light*, including typesetting and lay-out, for around $385, a sum of money that was nevertheless difficult for hippies living in bucolic poverty to raise.

Today Huffstickler remains at base a mystical, unorthodox but religious poet. He is the rare kind of religious poet who questions and does not demand a belief in a creator. Reading Huffstickler is good for your soul. Huff is a poet who does not write for other poets but writes for people who might enjoy

Why I Write in Coffee Houses and Diners

poetry. He is one of the few poets I know who has built a large following publishing nationally poem by poem in the small magazines, chapbook by chapbook, many done by small presses, many done by himself. He is a poet in love with the magical calling of poetry who is sustained by the writing itself rather than by dreams of fame or money.

Albert has been writing so long and so constantly that he has built up a huge corpus of work—much published, much unpublished—that it is heartening to see him coming full circle, from his first his first small-press book in 1979 to his first association with the publishing wonders of the World Wide Web.

Chuck Taylor

Texas A&M University

Introduction

Albert Huffstickler once observed in an interview I conducted for *The Sow's Ear Poetry Review* that his literary influences are many, and he counts visual and performing artists as inspirations. Early passions include the works of Thomas Wolfe, Ray Charles, and Edward Hopper. Coffee houses and diners—and the roads that take Huffstickler to and from them—also belong on this list of influences. Within these environs Huffstickler has chronicled a slice of twentieth-century life that will remain of interest to social historians as well as critics, poets, and general readers in years to come.

"I am a poet and artist," Huffstickler says in *Holy Secrets: The Art and Poetry of Albert Huffstickler*, a film by Matthew D. Listiak. "And an observer of humanity...from a safe distance." Then he laughs. His poems embody his observations and, often, his sense of humor. Imagine a man gift is limited only by the amount of time it takes to put words on paper. This is Huffstickler. He watches, and he writes.

Huffstickler's identification is, he admits, with the less fortunate. "I write about the outcasts a lot," he continues in *Holy Secrets*. "I think I was outside most of my life one way or the other."

As an outsider, Huffstickler is most at home in the small press community where his poems have received great acclaim. Since the 1970s, they have been published widely in the United States. Recently, they have begun to appear internationally and in translation. A prolific writer, Huffstickler makes few distinctions between prestigious academic journals that publish him and small, often handmade journals that keep his words in print and in the hands and ears of many. While he publishes books and chapbooks with small presses, he also continues to publish chapbooks under his own Press of Circumstance

Why I Write in Coffee Houses and Diners

imprint, selling these to people in the neighborhood close to home, to a scattered readership, and to university collections farther away.

In an introduction to a chapbook he published of Huffstickler's poems, under the Jamming Staplers Press imprint, James Rossignol paid tribute to Huffstickler's unabashed lack of pretension in his poetry. Although Huffstickler is well schooled, having earned a degree in English and having read widely in the canons of "great" and other literature, Rossignol noted that "you won't find him studying Persian poetry of the Golden Era to be writing later an Americanized imitation. You'll find him sitting on a park bench. You'll find him swirling the coffee grounds lying on the bottom of a styrofoam cup, contemplating them as one would tea leaves. You'll find him watching washing machines go round and round in a laundromat. You'll hear Huff's voice."

Chuck Taylor, an early publisher of Huffstickler's work with Slough Press, has said, "He is the quiet poet of coffee shops observing. In his later years another voice has become stronger, that of the modest sage poet telling the reader what he has learned by hard experience in life." It was this debt to coffee houses and diners that first led me to choose poems for this collection, but it was "Huff's voice" that convinced me that the poems I chose from the array of his work that I have collected over the years were the best way to introduce him to a mainstream audience.

I believe that Huffstickler's contribution to poetry is a significant one that will lead to more acclaim among readers and literary scholars in the future, but his poems deserve a wider readership now. Even if you have not heard him read aloud, you will hear his voice in the poems that follow. Naomi Shihab Nye says that Huffstickler "wears language / like comfortable clothes." Her poem "Huff," written for tribute to Huffstickler orchestrated by the Austin International Poetry Festival in 1997, calls Huffstickler a "citizen of the roads / crisscrossing human spirit's land."

Albert Huffstickler

Huffstickler's voice is strong, I think, because it gains its sustenance from the voices that he carries in his head from his quiet study of people. If you listen carefully, you will find that the existential loneliness to which Huffstickler witnesses transmutes into a sense of community of communion and peace. "The peace of loneliness be with you," begins "A Blessing Poem," which ends, "for in your loneliness you are not alone." There are many voices in his head, as he is a listener; alone, he is not alone. As he moves from coffee house to diner, to library, to home, he always carries his notebook, which sketches the poems that end up in his typewriter, still alive with the feelings and voices of the streets from which he has returned. Writer Mark Smith, in "Poem for Huff," reminds us, "He writes in a spiral bound book, coiling together past and future."

The strong voice that grows out of his crisscrossing of human spirit's land is what draws his readers, including other poets, to Huffstickler's poetry. Steven de Frates, in a poem entitled "Huffstickler" published in *Concho River Review*, notes that Huffstickler's poems "start in the middle / of things, then amble through / the labyrinth." "Armageddon," which recounts a surreal experience hitchhiking through Kentucky, is but one leg of the labyrinth. "October 31, 1985" is another. And there are more.

A journey motif is strong in Huffstickler's poetry, both within individual poems and across his body of work. Poet W. Joe Hoppe recognizes that and writes,

> We ride those Robert Frost roads
>
> Huff and me
>
> and come to a road not taken
>
> Huff plows straight off into the ditches
>
> bumping along my bag gets caught up
>
> in the motorcycle's monstrous rear wheel

Why I Write in Coffee Houses and Diners

belongings burst and scatter

flannel and plaid on the dry ditch grass

But Huff won't slow down

Based on a dream 2/18/94, typed up 2/20/94, "Dream Tour with Albert Huffstickler" honors Huffstickler's indefatigable quest to keep going, to keep writing, to keep his poems out there for others to read. Huffstickler's journeys in this book are found in poems such as "Armageddon" and "What It Means to be Free."

Someone who keeps going and is always watching is by default an outsider. Keddy Outlaw, poet and former editor of *Arrowsmith*, calls Huffstickler an "Honorary Outlaw." She has said, "He writes from that outside Outlaw place, and his words walk the streets of Outlaw loneliness." "Thanksgiving 1985" depicts this loneliness and tempers it with a settled sense of self and direction. In addition, De Frates has likened Huffstickler to the homeless, people who are on a journey with no clear end: "Like a lot of good poets, / he could be mistaken for / one of the homeless." In his poem "Doppleganger," Huffstickler recognizes himself in a homeless face. He gives freely to others, "tithing fate." Many of his poems are based on encounters with the homeless, in words that offer dignity and compassion.

The journey also becomes a way to explore the tensions of being lost and found, important tensions related to Huffstickler's existential sense of loneliness. "The Search" asks how people find each other. "I've been looking all my life." "Found" shows, ironically, that it is not possible to be lost. Moments of intimacy are found with intimate friends and with strangers, with father and mother, with the staff of places like Jane's Restaurant and the Cafe du Jour, where Huffstickler goes to write poems and drink coffee because "they know me here." Huffstickler's poems show that it is possible to be simultaneously lost and found, lonely and connected, here and not here.

Albert Huffstickler

All his time on benches, in coffee houses, in diners—and on the road—has given Huffstickler a gift of insight that he shares in his poems. While his poems emerge from his sense of self, his voice, they are not self absorbed. He recognizes the existential journeys of others and reminds us of the transience of life while marking small events such as somebody's stop at a bus shelter in "Markings" or the prophecies one might find in graffiti in "The Search." "Queen of the Royal Castle" recognizes the significance of a mundane trip in the life of his mother and shows yet again how Huffstickler takes the ordinary and makes it extraordinary, even mythical.

In his figurative and literal quests, Huffstickler has spent a good bit of time pondering what women have to offer him. Whereas Odysseus had Athena, Kirke, and Penelope, Huffstickler has also entertained a variety of muses, from friends to bag ladies to lovers to realistic figments of his imagination. The "Oracle" he finds in a food court is an interesting contrast with the mythical crone he creates in "Mandate from the Hag." His essential isolation is reinforced in the portrait of a seductive young women presented in "Quandary," whereas a fear of being trapped is presented in "Entrapment," a poem about being the object of a seduction.

The poems in this collection offer insight into the role of poetry and how it both anchors Huffstickler and sets him free, just as his readers will find anchors and be set free. "The Lost Poem" tells about how Huffstickler's father spent four years as a prisoner-of-war with a poem he revered in his pocket, a poem he continued to keep close when he returned home. The lost poem remains a point of connection with his father, and with readers. "It's a nice thought anyway," Huffstickler writes, "my poem in someone's pocket." Within his poems, we find that he memorializes people like his father and offers wisdom that will help people get through whatever they are getting through.

"Ministry" recognizes women Huffstickler remembers from a number of restaurants. He muses, "I wonder if they ever got back half as much as they gave." Wondering that about Huffstickler himself, it is impossible to do justice to his complete opus in a small preface. Future treatments of his work will

Why I Write in Coffee Houses and Diners

want to follow through on analysis of his themes and images, especially his use of the ordinary to present the extraordinary to evoke a sense of isolated communion. Within the simplest of settings, Huffstickler's poetry offers us great intimations of connectedness and peace and meaning.

Why I Write in Coffee Houses and Diners offers a small selection of poems from Huffstickler's published and unpublished work. While my goal with this collection is to introduce Huffstickler to a wider audience, I should also recognize the real reason the poems deserve more readers. Jay Woodman wrote in "Tiny," an essay published in *Rustic Rub* and dedicated to Huffstickler, "Poets belong everywhere, and may succeed in being everywhere by virtue of their work. It is not the name that matters, or the personality. What matters is the slow spread of what needs to be said. Tiny, the words slip into works. And the works slip into existence." Albert Huffstickler knows what needs to be said, and I welcome you to a selection of his words.

Felicia Mitchell

Emory & Henry College

The peace of loneliness be with you

The peace of corner booths in coffee shops

by highways a thousand miles from home

The peace of old fabric and ancient wood

and the peace of stone which knows only itself

The peace of churches and silent houses

and the peace of grass newly mown

Albert Huffstickler

The Way of Art

It seems to me that
paralleling the paths of action, devotion, etc.,
there is a path called Art
and that the sages of the East would recognize
Faulkner, Edward Hopper, Beethoven, William
    Carlos Williams,
and address them as equals.
It's a matter of intention and discipline, isn't
    it?—
combined with a certain God-given ability.
It's what you're willing to go through, willing to
    give, isn't it?
It's the willingness to be a window
through which others can see
all the way out to infinity
and all the way back to themselves.

Condition

I continue in place.
The autumn grows.
The days go down beneath
my measured tread.
Some days I question everything.
Some days I'm so silent
not a leaf stirs when I pass.
I could be stone.
I think as a stone
and there is that in me
that asks for nothing.
My days pile up
like stones in a field.
I make no effort to arrange them.
The seasons and the elements
will shape them in their time.
Meanwhile,
I continue in place,
dreaming my stone dreams.
The autumn grows.
Nights, the wind
moves through the darkness
like a living shadow.

Albert Huffstickler

Meditation in Wyatt's

It's been over a year now
since I had my mystical experience
sitting among the old folks in Wyatt's Cafeteria
eating my fried chicken,
over a year since I saw those silver lines
extending from my heart to every person in
    the room,
linking us.
And knew that those lines existed in another
    dimension
and that those lines were poetry.
Now, I sit here in the same place once again
and the old folks are moving through the
    serving line
or seated over their dinners chatting in their flat,
    small voices.
There's a resonance in the room
and those silver lines are moving between us as
    before.
And watching them I know
that poetry has a subtle existence
that is prior to any word, sound, meaning,
prior to anything now existing.
(An old man at the next table
bends double, coughing,
then straightens with a gasp
and the talk goes on.)

Coffee House Poets

They like to write
where people are.
They like a little noise
with their silence.
They want to look up
and see something.
They want to be surprised.
They like the flow
of bodies around them.
Or perhaps it's just loneliness—
yes, that too.
But more than that:
they like the atmosphere
a little smoke laden.
The like aromas—
coffee, tobacco, meat frying.
They like the sudden revelation
as eyes look off
or blur with tears
looking across a table.
Where others court eternity,
they're in love with the moment
in all its tawdriness and glory,
that instant when truth appears
out of nowhere—a truth
as simple and as natural
as people sitting together
in a room over coffee
in all their vulnerability
and their humanness.

Albert Huffstickler

Déjà Vu

She is the Sixties—
long straight hair,
far-off look,
the casual way she
fits into her body.
She serves my coffee
every day
at the snack bar.
Today I told her,
"You remind me of
the Sixties."
"Oh, I was just a
a little girl back then."
Coming back slowly,
handing me my change,
all the time in the world.
The whole of existence
a kind of background
music to her dreaming.
No wonder we believed.

The Visitation

She said she was the Madonna of
Ancient Sorrows, here to redeem
men from themselves. Her rags
were a disguise, she told me,
because she worked purely by
telepathy. She was beautiful
in the way that old things are
beautiful, burnished and scarred
but glowing still as old things
glow sometimes as though their
very age created a luster that
youth could never emulate. She
stood there in the mouth of the
alley silent then raised her arms
in blessing. The rags parted
to reveal a small, round
perfect breast then the starlight
gathered on the point of the
tiny nipple and a moment later
she was gone. A stray cat,
thin as hope, ran across my feet
and vanished into the darkness
while I stood on.

Albert Huffstickler

Doppleganger

Beside the dumpster
at Ruta Maya
stands a man who
looks like me.
I always give him
money—tithing fate.

Why I Write in Coffee Houses and Diners

Rainbow Grill, Downtown Austin

Skin knows.
It drinks morning light.
Wine of the flesh.
Seated by the window,
I absorb it
with my morning coffee,
thinking how like love it is.
Wine of the flesh
Wine of the soul
Remembrance of clarity

Albert Huffstickler

Parameters

Within the circle of this room
(and all rooms are circles)
the little old lady
who has a Persian cat at home
(I know she does)
sits beneath her dyed hair smiling.
She has a secret.
She knows we're on the wrong planet
but she isn't telling anyone—
not even the friend at whom
she smiles so intimately
over her coffee cup.
It is a grave secret,
a grave responsibility.
She sits amid the seawash of voices
holding her secret, stroking it
as she strokes her Persian cat.
And this is not a shopping mall
at all but a space ship.

Why I Write in Coffee Houses and Diners

The waves of space wash over us,
the spray flecking our faces
with tiny dots of cold.
"And your kids grow up
and get married and leave,"
says the woman at the next table.
Our ship plunges, rights itself,
and plunges on,
breasting the waves of space.
The little old lady
nods her dyed head and smiles,
stroking her secret.
And on what new planet
will our ship set down?
And will it be home?

Albert Huffstickler

Father and Daughter

She looks at him
from the corner of her eye,
a shy glance upward,
fourteen or so.
Her features are his
but her eyes lustrous:
his seem dead
and he bends beneath
the burden of her adoration.
She eats a corndog,
sips a coke,
and observes him gently
from the corner of her eye,
all delicacy
poised over her corndog
as over
her imminent womanhood.
He is the traveler come back
with his burden of horror
and despair.
She is the journeyer forth.
What can he say to her?
His brow furrows.
The too-old face contorts.
She observes him without comment,
at peace.
Nothing can touch her
while she's beside him
and he,
for once in his life,
is adequate.

Mother and Daughter

Facing each other
across the table
locked in their secrets,
the blood beat of
the loins ignored.
Their words are casual.
Their eyes move away.
There is a pulsing and
a silence between them,
something primitive.
They could be framed
in palm leaves.
Something tropical and
lush surrounds them.
Daughter arches her back.
Her young breasts
rise and fall.
Her loins grip the chair.
The jungle heat
surrounds her.
Mother leans forward
about to speak,
sighs, sits back,
looks off again.
The pulsing and
the silence grow as,
locked in their
womb-dark secrets,
they sit on.

Albert Huffstickler

Trial by Fire

Loneliness is a cold flame
that flays the soul.
When you pass through the fire
you know things then
no mortal man should know.
You're Lazarus come from the dead
living among men with
your death still on you,
knowing too much to ever have a friend,
a broken building with the lights left on
sagged against the sky, mortally wounded.
You'd thought that by enduring
You'd come to peace and reconciliation,
warm hands.
You come instead to a place
where no one's been
and stand in the starless night
hands to your face
and no strength left,
lost from man and unknown to God
and no way back.
It's then you know
you must make a place for yourself
of dry bones and anguish,
wring light from the substance of your will
and hope from the bone-dry earth.
It's then you know
that the only chance you stand
is to forge a star
out of your living breath.

Why I Write in Coffee Houses and Diners

A Ritual Song of Parting

After all the goodbyes
and the silences after;
after thinking about all
the things that don't work anymore,
think then of stone
and wood and durability
and then of how
there is a quality of grace
in a relationship
that is its underpinning,
that keeps you from
bumping into each other
when you walk and from
saying the word that
can't be taken back—
a quality that makes
drinking a cup of coffee
together an occasion
when a banquet with someone else
would be nothing.
And remind yourself that
when that quality of grace is gone
the parting has already taken place
and whatever
you were meant to do together
is done.

Albert Huffstickler

At the Cafe Du Jour

They know me here.
They know what I want and bring it.
When I write a check,
they don't ask for identification.
(Last night I watched the pecan leaves
fade and blacken into darkness
from my bedroom window.
They're yellowing finally this warm autumn
and will be gone soon.)
Felicia is shopping the Mall
and left me to sit here drinking coffee.
This is my Saturday place.
Across the room,
a woman cradles a sleeping child
and sips coffee with her free hand.
Next month I'll be 57.
It's hard sometimes not to feel betrayed.
By what?
Time or that unknown person,
usually designated parent,
who should have told me—
told me what?
That the years are passing
and that the aging process
is not a gradual thing
but a single sudden shock
repeated over and over until
we no longer resist it.
Yesterday I visited Wanda at the retirement home
and watched the old folks eat Thanksgiving
      dinner.

Why I Write in Coffee Houses and Diners

They looked so bewildered.
It came to me that we have lost
any talent we have for growing old and drying.
We only know how to be young
and watch t.v.
It's like knowing how to say hello
but not being able to say goodbye.
It's the goodbye that links us.
The hello is momentary and spasmodic
but the goodbye is graceful and eternal.
We need to learn that again.

Albert Huffstickler

Entrapment

Trapped by my needs—
come on to by a seventy-plus-year-old woman
in the Cafe du Jour.
She talked for forty-five minutes
with sly allusions to sex,
me feeling more and more ancient and
      uncomfortable.
Oh, she read me right,
I was lonely—
but not that lonely—yet.
On and on as though
only her small shrill voice held back
that wall of impending existential isolation,
a bright voice but breaking slightly,
on and on till I wanted to yell,
"O.K.! I surrender!" but I didn't,
just let her run on and on
till the silence finally
could stand it no longer
and lowered itself like a warm, damp curtain
over us, smothering everything,
whereupon she rose, excused herself brightly
with the promise of seeing me again
and bounced out
trailing behind her the bright, tattered fragments
of a long life
like the banner of a once-great army
silent before its impending doom.

Why I Write in Coffee Houses and Diners

Quandary

    I'm glad she moved.
    Her dress kept sliding
    off her shoulder and
    I couldn't take my eyes away.
    Something inside me
    kept fluttering open
    and I was engulfed by
    tenderness. Well,
    you get strange when
    you've been alone too
    long, I told myself.
    But it went deeper
    than that. You see,
    I loved her for that
    one patch of skin
    that took the light
    just so. And if love
    can spring from such
    inconsequentials,
    then what hope is there?

Albert Huffstickler

What You Will, or Love Among the Chicken Soup

I thought I saw you standing among the broccoli
    at HEB's,
greenish, head drooping to the side, arms
    akimbo—
but you were really behind the chicken soup at
    the Minimax,
brow furrowed with concentration as you strove
    to look cylindrical.
Only later did I realize that you were the third
    croissant on the left
at the Cafe du Jour, curled semi-foetally with
    fingers and toes pointed
and looking quite flaky, which explains the
    success of your deception.
That's when it came to me that you tend to see
    what you want in this world,
which led me to digressions into what perception
    really is,
the nature of reality and the cosmic implications
of too many visits to shopping malls.
Whereupon I decided that there had to be more
    purpose to my life,
which is how I came to take you off the shelf of
    Waldenbooks,
looking fiercely oblong and paginated (title:
    *What To Tell Your
Child About Reincarnation*) and went home to
    catch up on my reading.

Secrecy

What took me so long to realize was
that what she talked about
was not what was on her mind.
She invariably sought me out in a crisis
then, often as not,
talked about the weather.
Later, I learned,
that if I guessed what was going on,
she was willing to discuss it
just as though she'd brought it up herself.
It had something to do with
childhood and secrecy—
surviving in an adult world.
She still had the voice and manner of a child.
Sometimes I wanted to take her
by the shoulders and shake her
and say, "But you made it.
Look around you. You're here!"
But it wouldn't have done any good
because somebody didn't make it
or there wouldn't have been
all those secrets.

Albert Huffstickler

Beliefs on Which We Stake Our Lives

It's Monday Morning
on Guadalupe Street
in Austin, Texas, and
I sit writing over coffee,
gazing out the broad
windows of Jane's Restaurant
at the morning traffic,
knowing that a street
is a drained river and
cars are boats with wheels.

Why I Write in Coffee Houses and Diners

Silent Night in Hyde Park

The lights are on in Quack's.
The bench is empty but
a single figure hunches over
a table. Dolce Vita hums.
Fresh Plus is closed. It's
after ten but the lights
glow and someone is moving
far back in the room. Manga
is full and on the parking lot
a group of women chatter and
laugh. And the night grows.
And I am moving through that
night feeling the pulse of
it, feeling the subtle current
that links these separate
things. A car pulls in to
Pronto Food Mart, more lights
crossing the darkness. This
night is nothing but ordinary.
These lights are just lights
and the stillness beneath it all
is just a stillness.

Albert Huffstickler

Old Acquaintance

He said, You look like
somebody I knew a
long time ago. But
you're probably not.
Besides, I think
He's dead. I said,
I think I know who
you mean and you're
right. I'm not
him. And yes, he
is dead.

Why I Write in Coffee Houses and Diners

The Plaza, Santa Fe

In the night, the plaza gleams
beneath the falling snow.
I sit watching from the Plaza Cafe
and know that this small square is sacred.
What saint's bones rest
beneath that frozen ground,
I do not know.
But they're there—
the last remains of a peaceful,
        gentle man
whose touch was like snowflakes
on your lifted face.

Albert Huffstickler

One of Those Times When Words Are Not Enough

I came here to Ruta Maya Coffee House
in the early morning Austin summer to write.
Now I sit here
and sit here
with the breeze on my face
watching and listening,
the fragrance of coffee and tobacco
flooding my space,
thinking I must be
the king of Ruta Maya and the king of Austin,
thinking how there's a silence to old brick
a stateliness to old brick buildings,
a containedness, a serenity—
as though they shared a secret
we could never understand.

Why I Write in Coffee Houses and Diners

The Way Things Come and Go

Taco Cabana, Monday morning,
huevos rancheros, 3 strips of bacon,
refried beans, 2 tortillas and coffee,
for $2.89. Beat that if you can.
Grey November morning, doctor's office.
Blood sugar up, back on medication.
Well, I fasted so they could take my blood
and now I break my fast at Taco Cabana
to make more blood so I'll be ready next time.
Meanwhile, Adios, Mexico sings the jukebox,
the voices blending,
that horny little trumpet keeping time.
Belly full, top off my coffee.
I'm back in business, making blood.

Albert Huffstickler

Report to Renee

Eight o'clock: I had cornflakes
for breakfast and coffee at the Hyde Park Bakery,
then caught the bus downtown
and bought some pipe tobacco
and had coffee at Texas French Bread,
where I wrote a poem about going to Santa Fe.
A transient came into the tobacco shop
and bought a pack of cigarettes on sale for 95¢.
He said he was saving a quarter
to call his friend because,
if they could each get a dollar,
they were going to the Night Hawk for coffee.
That sounded all right to me.
Then I caught the Red River bus
to Hancock Center and shopped for groceries,
walked home, ate, and took a nap,
walked down Avenue G to a yard sale
where I bought three short-sleeved shirts
for 50¢ apiece and a toaster for $2.
Then I went home and tried the toaster out.
Only one side works.
I ate a piece of toast.
I forgot to say that earlier this morning I had
coffee with Hester, my 76-year-old neighbor
whose daughter yells so loud
I can't even talk to my company some evenings.
I also forgot to say that my dishwasher
was broken and when the landlord came by
I told him about it and when
I got home from town it was fixed. So I
washed my dishes.

Why I Write in Coffee Houses and Diners

Lonely people stay busy, have you noticed?
Anyway, by now it was very hot
and I took a bath, closed my house
and lay down with the air conditioner on
and read till I fell asleep.
I did not dream about you.
I've decided that I have to start
dreaming about older women
since you are never going to grow up
in time for me.
Hester has a parakeet.
Now it's late afternoon. I walk across
the street to have coffee with Daniel,
the manager of the Hyde Park Bakery.
We talk awhile.
Later, I go home and fix supper: hamburger steak,
salad, corn, a jalapeño pepper and a pear for
    dessert.
By then, it is eight o'clock
and getting dark and I'm lonesome
so I walk over here to Burch's Restaurant
where I get coffee and sit writing this to say
that when you get older you'll understand
how people get lonely for someone to share
    their day
as I'm sharing mine with you. There's a
thing called intimacy, a very scarce commodity
in this world of busy people.
It's a feeling like tiny hands reaching
inside you to hold and stroke your heart.

Albert Huffstickler

Arby's Brenda

> "In the battle of life,
> nobody gets any medals."

I'm not really sure I could live with happy people.
The small, middle-aged woman across from me
      on the bus
wears an Arby's nametag.
Her name is Brenda and she wears the bright,
impossible smile of lonely people everywhere,
that smile that's both an invitation to kindness
and a shield against rejection, a smile much like
      my own.
I think of all the middle-aged people in the world
who work at fast food places and ride the bus
      home evenings.
I think of small cluttered rooms with black and
      white TVs
and windows overlooking an alley,
how we never think of pale, middle-aged people
who work in fast food places dying of love
or nursing secret ambitions to be president
or fly a jet, be a movie star or write a bestseller.
The truth is (and here's the tragedy)
we never think of these people at all.

Why I Write in Coffee Houses and Diners

In fact, I wouldn't be surprised if it weren't
 possible
for a person to live out his whole life
without giving a moment's thought
to a single middle-aged employee of a fast food
 place anywhere.
Now tell me this: Is it just me or doesn't it seem
 to you
that there's something impossibly wrong
 somewhere?

Albert Huffstickler

I Dreamed I Lived in Austin

I dreamed I lived in Austin.
I was fifty-four
with legs like a sparrow
and a hungry heart.
I was looking for God
but kept finding people—
strange little people
with pieces of their bodies missing:
an arm, a leg, a nose, a belly button.
They kept offering me ham sandwiches
and telling me I was going to die.
I'd already died, I told them,
chewing mightily and wishing I
        had some water.
That was just a preview, they said.
Next time, you'll *really* die.
And they marched ahead of me,
flip-flop, as I combed the streets
searching for God.

Suddenly it was night
and I was standing on the edge of town
alone.
A cold moon shone over me
and the lights of a little cafe
gleamed down the road.
An old man wobbled up to me and said,
"Well, here I am."
"God?" I asked.
"Who else? Got a quarter?"
"Yes." I gave it to him.

Why I Write in Coffee Houses and Diners

"Let's make it to that diner," he said.
"Refills are free.
I'll tell you anything you want."
"For just a quarter?" I asked.
God chuckled. "Got a cigarette?"
I gave him one.
We made it to the Cafe and ordered coffee,
hunched in a booth in the warm room,
the lights soft and comforting.
"Anything special you want?" God asked,
taking another cigarette from the pack
and lighting it with my Bic.
"Love," I sad. I started to cry.
"O.K.," he said, patting my arm
with a boney hand.
The room vanished and once more
I was in Austin. I was fifty-four
with legs like a sparrow
and a hungry heart.

She stood before me, eyes
        misty and tender.
"God sent me," she said.
"I know."
She offered me a ham sandwich
and told me I was going to die.
"But not for a while," she said
and took my arm.
"Good enough," I said.
"I'm not going to die for a while,
I have you,
and God owes me a quarter
and two cigarettes and"—

Albert Huffstickler

I felt in my pockets—
"a Bic lighter.

Would you like to hear
what I dreamed last night?"
"Yes."
"Well, I dreamed I lived in Austin.
I was fifty-four
with legs like a sparrow
and a hungry heart.
I was looking for God
but kept finding people."
"And love," she added.
"Yes, love," I agreed.
"I think it's a set," she said.

Why I Write in Coffee Houses and Diners

Nostrum

Some days I just let
        everything go
and sink into the neighborhood,
sit on the bench
        in front of the bakery,
talk to anyone that passes
and don't think about
        anything at all.
I think they call that
        healing.

Albert Huffstickler

Sanctuary

We pulled into Aspen on a winter's evening,
dark coming in, heavy clouds threatening snow.
It was time to find a warm place,
curl up and drink coffee—which we did
at the first bright window we came to,
called Jim to come and get us,
then sat in the warm room sipping,
feeling the dark grow out there
like some giant creature from another planet,
self spawning, indestructible,
but powerless within our magic square of light.

Christmas Lights

I'll never be a real Christian.
I can't love the world—just individuals.
But that night driving around Houston
with the lights gleaming in the yards,
the great buildings downtown bordered in lights,
light spraying at us from all directions—
that night I thought I'd touched something
so deep, so central that I *could* love the world—
or most of it. But of course it was
just that we were together and that holiness
I felt was right in the car
with us and that was fine.
So I thought, "Well, maybe that's how you get
      there—
by loving one person at a time
until you love all of them.
If so, then this looks like
a good place to start."

Albert Huffstickler

Grill Smoke

The smoke from the grill is dusk blue and thick
    like rope
and sometimes, standing beside Howard,
who drags a worn towel across the blue-yellow
    surface
        of its face,
wiping it roughly as a woman will scrub a
    child's mouth
        with a lipsticked kleenex—
sometimes when the thick ropes crawl leisurely,
pathetically patient, up through the vents
like old, crippled men scrambling up a hillside,
I feel myself moving, crawling with them,
and grip the bright chrome handle of the cof-
    fee urn
to hold myself back
for fear that I'll go after them,
hobble out into the night,
and vanish on the wind.

Why I Write in Coffee Houses and Diners

An End to Mourning

Loneliness stands on the corner
waiting for a handout.
The book of love
has all the pages torn.
The weatherman says rain today
but what does he know?
We'll be born again like flowers,
mindless as flowers,
entranced by our own beauty
while in the sepulchres of alleys
the beggar kneels
before an altar of broken windows.
His prayers rise up
like smoke from ancient fires as
along the back streets of the heart,
the blind man taps a cosmic semaphore
and all the lights in the city
go out at once.

Albert Huffstickler

Ranch House Restaurant, Burnet, Texas

What we needed was bacon and eggs and biscuits
and that was what we got.
Dark grace of morning coffee,
absolving night and its foment.
Keen country faces,
sound of voices long familiar to each other
exploring familiar subjects,
brown, rich light reflected from paneled walls.
It's ritual—this morning convocation:
the hand on the shoulder,
the greeting, the exchange, the departure—
subdued ritual befitting the participants,
indigenous, eschewing display:
the ritual of the beginning of the day.

Why I Write in Coffee Houses and Diners

Claude

Claude Walker
old saw-filer
in his sixties
wept drunk
in my arms
for his dead
granddaughter
slobbering
fly open
stinking and
weeping who
downed double
shots like
sody pop
and worked a
sixteen-hour
day still drunk
from the night
before at sixty-
three: wept
in my arms
for a dead
child him-
self immune
to mortality.

Albert Huffstickler

What It Means to Be Free

We forget
till the bus to New Mexico
stops at the Kettle
in Del Rio at midnight
and we troop out
strangers
half-asleep
to mingle with the natives
order hamburgers
and coffee
crouch in a booth
eating and watching
safe in the knowledge
that no one knows
your name.
Finished, sitting back
to light a cigarette
watch the old cowboy
stomp up to the counter
couple in a corner
making shy love.
You bless them from
your magnificent distance
order a second
cup to go
then amble out
to the star-crisp night
stand looking up
then climb aboard.
The engine revs.
You glide off.

Why I Write in Coffee Houses and Diners

Lighting a cigarette
you sip your coffee
lean back
watching the night
stroke past
contained
content:
for this moment
there's nothing you need.

Albert Huffstickler

Quinlen's Promise

What came to Quinlen finally
sitting on a bus at night somewhere
between home and Santa Fe (one of
the periodic pilgrimages he made
all though this time) was the Donut
Theory. People were like donuts: there
was always a hold in the middle. If
you found yourself, came to know
who you were, the hole was still
there. It was implicit. To know
mortality was to know loss. It
was in the contract. Because
when you were made, a part of you
was left with God and must be
redeemed in person. We will never
be completely at home here because
a part of us was never here in the
first place. Quinlen knew that
this was his final revelation and
took it into him and held it. And
as he did, all questions ceased
and he was not more and no less than
he had been before. He was Quinlen
on a bus moving through the darkness.
When the night ended, he would be
in Santa Fe, basking in the clear
eternal light.

Why I Write in Coffee Houses and Diners

Bus at Night

This would be
a good time to die—now
speeding down the road at night
in this red and silver shell
not knowing anyone,
all the unwritten words
lulled to sleep
by the sound of the road
moving under me.
I could just
close my eyes
and drift off,
unwatched by any clocks,
uncounted
or counted only
by the uncounting stars.

Albert Huffstickler

Looking at the Ground

I've noticed lately
that, after 15 years on the same job,
I don't look at the ground so much anymore.
You see, when you're broke, you're always look-
    ing at the ground.
This is not due to humility.
It's because you're always looking for things,
things that other people have dropped or
    thrown away—
money first, of course, but also cigarettes,
like a half-empty pack that someone has
    dropped or discarded
(in more desperate straits, a long butt),
refundable pop bottles, aluminum cans,
anything that shines or beckons to be used again.
Life is a perpetual treasure hunt when you're
    broke.
Maybe, underneath it all, you're really looking
    for redemption
but for the time being you'll settle for
anything that's spendable, edible or smokeable.
Once I found a billfold lying on the ground by a
    self-service Post Office.
Good citizen that I am, I carefully extracted the
    cash ($35)
and dropped the wallet in the mail slot.
It was like unemployment insurance.
I didn't have to go to Manpower for 3 days.
My mother used to say, "The Lord takes cares of
    fools and drunks."

Why I Write in Coffee Houses and Diners

I don't think he takes such good care of poor
    people.
They're on their own.
Eyes on the ground, eternally searching for the
    next good thing,
that thing that will spell security for a minute or
    an hour,
a cup of coffee in a diner and, with luck, a ciga-
    rette to smoke with it,
the warmth of a lighted room purchased at the
    price of your last 50¢.
It's the cold you fear—and those long, empty
    spaces.
So you walk along looking at the ground, fol-
    lowing an invisible trail
down streets, up alleys, across parking lots and on,
moving with that patient, solemn shuffle
that's the universal gait of the poor man—
eyes on the ground, that little piece of ground
    right in front of his feet,
the only piece of earth in this whole world
he can call his own.

Albert Huffstickler

Wayfarer

She said she did not remember,
standing on the corner
with the lights flashing.
She said that all the roses had died
as the earth grew dry and parched
and the sun blazed.
She told me how she held the dry petals
carefully in her cupped hands
till they crumbled into dust
then walked away.
She said she did not remember
and was not going back
and they would never find her
because she was invisible
standing there on the corner
with the lights flashing
and that I was invisible too
or I would not be able to see her.

Why I Write in Coffee Houses and Diners

Blood and Roses

She told me that roses drank
blood—at least the red ones
and the pink ones did, that's
where the color came from but
the pink ones didn't get enough.
She said that it was the roots
that crept into your house at
night, wriggling along like
snakes or worms till they came
to your bed and then they
fastened their little feelers
to you and drained your blood
only sometimes if you started
to wake up, they'd let go and
leave before you saw them.
That's why some were pink. They
Hadn't gotten through eating.
She said she woke up one night
and didn't move a muscle, didn't
even open her eyes and she
felt them there, that's how
she knew, one of them was wrapped
around her ankle and she could
feel it sucking. The next
morning she looked out in her
yard and there was a big new
bloom on her rose bush just
like that. How much proof do
you need? she asked.

Albert Huffstickler

Starburn

He said he'd slept out
so much this year he'd
gotten a bad case of
starburn. "Starburn?" "Yeah,
you know. Those stars
can burn you. I mean
all over but especially
when they get in your
head. They itch, Man."
"I see," I said. "You've
got a bad case of starburn
in your head." "Not just
my head, Man. All over.
But it's better now. I've
been sleeping at the
Sally the last couple of
weeks. It's cleared up
now, almost gone. Do
you see any starburn
anywhere?" "Not a bit," I
told him. "Yeah!" he said.
He shouldered his backpack
and walked off nodding to
himself. "I think
the worst is over."

Why I Write in Coffee Houses and Diners

Madman on the Corner

And if I once got into your mind
how would I ever get out?
And if I felt for a moment your despair
and it erupted from my lips
in a torrent of unspeakable rage
and overwhelming sorrow,
would it ever stop?

Albert Huffstickler

Waiting for Sylvia

I am working on an equation
for measuring friendships in coffee cups.
This certainly must be a thousand-cup friendship
after lo these twenty-some years.
But there's another way you could go about it.
You could do a diagram of a friendship
by charting the locations of the coffee shops
    you've met in.
I think of the Chuckwagon, the Tower
    Restaurant,
the Diary Queen across from the Ching Wong
    Laundry,
a tidy, old-fashioned place in North Troy,
    Vermont,
that I can't remember the name of,
the Cafe du Jour, the Cactus Cafe on campus,
the Sundae Palace on Duval Street,
the Rexall, the Night Hawk, Uncle Van's,
The Plantation, the Red River Cafe.
There's a chronology working here also
but that's another dimension.
So what comes of all this coffee, all these cups?

Why I Write in Coffee Houses and Diners

Perhaps there's a dark brown essence
that distills over the years,
a rich, vibrant brown glow
that pervades two people's auras when they
    come together
and blends them into one person
and this is what is described as friendship.
It's something to think about.
But here she comes.
We'll talk about it later.

Albert Huffstickler

Coffee

Coffee is the great comforter.
I try to catch everyone
especially in the early morning.
A lot of the patients can't
have anything, of course, but
the people that brought them can
and often they had to leave home
without that first fragrant cup.
It's something you can do that's
quick and warm and comforting
and it's something you can
bring to them so that they feel
cared for. That's a lot.
If you really want appreciation
try bringing a cup of coffee
to someone who's had to get up
and bring a friend or loved one
here and is worried and afraid
and maybe still half asleep
and trying to be there for someone
when they're not there for themselves.
I don't know about you but
science is going to have to
come up with a lot more evidence
before I'll believe that
a good cup of coffee is
anything but a blessing.

Why I Write in Coffee Houses and Diners

The Lost Diner

Oh, I know it's an illusion
that I could sit somewhere in a diner
smoking and drinking coffee and write forever.
In the first place,
there's only so much coffee I can drink
and after a while I get restless
or have to pee and some days
for all my love of people,
I don't want to see anyone at all,
just hide away in my room
preferably in bed with the covers
pulled up to the top of my head.
So I know it's an illusion—
that mythical 24 hour place
shining in the night beside a highway
with the booths just right
and the stainless steel gleaming
and the waitress always at my elbow
with the next refill and the words
pouring out of me in an endless stream
till I'm finally dry and whole.
Yes, it's all allusion, myth.
But I'll tell you what:
I'd like to try it. I'd like for somebody
just to hand me the money and say, "O.K.
Take off. There's the road.
And every time you come to a diner,
just stop and have yourself a cup
of coffee and write a poem."
How long would I last? I don't know.

Albert Huffstickler

But I'll bet you this:
I'd know more about this country
than I do now.
And I'd bring back a book with a Formica cover
and every time you picked it up,
you'd smell bacon frying
and the brown fragrance of coffee
and you'd hear the roar of those big diesels
singing in your ears like all the lost angels
in the universe come home at once.

Why I Write in Coffee Houses and Diners

At Wyatt's Cafeteria

I love to watch that little old lady smoke.
She enjoys it so much,
puffing away at her long cigarette,
dragging it in while she talks
across the empty plates to her friend.
She must be eighty,
fine-featured, neatly groomed,
puffing away.
If she ever feared cancer,
it was long ago.
Now, there's just the pure enjoyment,
the sweet residue,
the pale smoke moving around her
like the mist above a wide river
in the morning light.

Albert Huffstickler

The Plaza Cafe, Santa Fe

The little Indian girl
with the Buster Brown bob
eats pancakes two stools down.
They are very good.
Her eyes shine.
She has hot chocolate
with whipped cream too.
And I have a poem.
We're both happy.

Why I Write in Coffee Houses and Diners

I Have a Dream

At McDonald's in the morning light,
golden arches, American flag:
platitudes of sunlight
like pansies in an old maid's flower bed.
Will the real George Washington stand up?
Embedded in the system, we twist and writhe,
struggling to clear our eyes.
Will the real Walt Whitman please stand?
What would you like on your Big Mac, Sir?
I dream my feet have disappeared
and I'm walking on the stumps to—
somewhere. I forget.
Trees lift and sway their branches
beyond the golden arches' myopic gleam.
The sunlight dapples them.
Clouds pass.
The sky is blue, pale blue.
And we have wandered to this place
out of the crumpled night
seeking comforts of coffee and solitude
by the dawn's early light.

Albert Huffstickler

To My Twin Born Dead

It was like being stuck in a door,
both of us fighting to get out,
the pressure building
like there was a crowd behind us
pushing, pushing.
And then a sudden surge
and I burst through,
hearing your voice trail away behind me
as I floundered out there in the light,
thinking, "The door was too small."
And later then they brought you out,
a battered lifeless thing,
and I was alone for the first time ever.

Sometimes I wonder
if all my poems are to you,
keeping a record you'll never read
of my sojourn in that place
you never reached.
Sometimes I think
they need to invent
a new word for loneliness—
a sound that reaches
into the marrow of the bone
then passes on
into infinity.

Heart Song

On the doorstep of your heart
a beggar stands.
It is yourself
wanting to get in.
It is very cold.
You've been gone a long time.
You do not think you'll be remembered.
You knock on the door.
The sound of your knocking
echoes and reechoes on the still air.
It is getting colder.
You wonder how long
you can stand here in the cold waiting.
The echo of your knocking dies
and there is silence all around you.
It is evening.
The night approaches.
You wonder where you will go,
who will take you in.
On the doorstep of your heart,
a beggar stands.
It is yourself.

Albert Huffstickler

Effort

It's all about effort
effort to meet the day,
effort to put one foot in front of the other,
effort to walk erect,
effort to support some intolerable and unknown
        burden,
effort to hold the eyes open,
effort to focus eyes and attention.
If we're intended to be in a body,
then why is everything so difficult?
Why is it like operating an unfamiliar and
recalcitrant machine—from the outside?
Effort to pray,
effort to believe there's somebody out there
hearing the prayer,
crazy enough to make a world like this
but sane enough to intervene.
Effort to hold back the darkness,
effort to hold back the darkness,
effort to hold back the darkness,
effort to…

Why I Write in Coffee Houses and Diners

Awaiting Clearance

I sit here in this room
over coffee, finished
but not wanting to
go outside. Something
in us always not
wanting to go outside,
putting it off.
Voices rise and fall,
plates rattle. The
light in the window
beckons. And I sit here
still, half entranced,
not wanting to stir,
not wanting to put
my pen away, not
wanting to go outside.

Albert Huffstickler

Puzzle

It's a jigsaw puzzle
but with more variables:
this piece fits that one
in color and shape
but here's another
that also fits.
Complete it one way,
It's square and looks
like a road leading
off across a desert.
Another version
is round and there's
a mountain
wreathed in clouds
pierced by starlight.
When the last piece
is in place,
the whole picture
comes apart
leaving you with
a new puzzle.
And less time.

Why I Write in Coffee Houses and Diners

October 31, 1981

Winter. Austin. 1964.
Bright windows steam-fogged
in coffee shops along the Drag,
love a mist rising from damp streets
to fog the air as,
chilled, you trudged homeward
hunched in your coat,
having sat anchored
in shop after shop
(The Night Hawk, Hank's,
The Rexall, The Pancake House)
sipping your coffee,
reading messages in the air
of those bright, warm rooms
and others in the lights
on winter streets as,
burrowed in your coat,
you peered out, animal-like.
Cosmic. It was all cosmic.
You see that now
walking those same streets,
the buildings just buildings,
the pavements flat black,
flashing no messages
in the lights of passing cars.
It was.
Now it's gone.

Albert Huffstickler

And you sit sipping your coffee
hunched and forlorn
like an old drunk seeking refuge
from night's violence
and winter's cold.

God!
Was love really here
and we missed it?
Or is it somewhere farther on?

Why I Write in Coffee Houses and Diners

Holidays, Holy Days

Sitting in Star's Cafe with Valerie late
    Thanksgiving night,
Valerie feeling the loneliness of the single parent
having just herded four children through the
    holiday—
coffee, me smoking, a stunnedness about us,
her seeing too many people that day, me not
    enough—
not wanting to talk now, just be with someone
    not having to talk,
that holiday despair on us, huddled together
    over coffee,
that despair that grows as the holiday draws to
    a close,
that terrible sorrow that says, "Well, you tried
    again
but you'll never get home."

Albert Huffstickler

Thanksgiving 1985

Some things need to be commemorated:
I was walking to Winchell's for coffee
when four old boys in a dark blue VW fastback
    pulled up.
"How ya doin?" asks the driver.
"Fine," I said.
"You wanta go smoke some dope and drink
    some beer and eat some turkey?"
"Thanks," I told him, "but I've got a place to go to."
"Well, we'll find somebody." They waved and
    wheeled off.
It was warm in Winchell's. Outside Autumn had
    finally arrived.
Somehow, as you grow older, each holiday
    becomes a day of reckoning.
One of the crazies is talking to his girl on the
    phone.
She doesn't seem very responsive.
His voice grows louder, more urgent.
Finally, he hangs up and stands there a moment
    shaking his head.
The room busies, then empties.
I finish my coffee and leave.
Walking home, a transient stops me, bums a
    cigarette
and asks if I know if the Salvation Army is still
    serving.
I can take a hint. I give him three dollars and
    walk on,
trying to decide whether that evens the score or
    not.

Why I Write in Coffee Houses and Diners

Shelter

Tres Piedras in the rain
(tiny town at the top of the world
in northern New Mexico).
Crouched at the counter
in the lone diner,
backpack in corner,
smoking,
nursing my coffee,
not wanting to go out
to that flat grey
that seemed endless
and the steady fall,
bite of the air.
Soul-damp and cautious,
I cupped the room's warmth to me,
sipped light with my coffee,
all the while laying
traps for my courage
along the borders of my mind.
A man without a home
is a different animal.
I stayed till the last drop
in my cup had vanished,
till the cup became a mirror
that I cared not to scan,
till there was no choice
but to go,

Albert Huffstickler

then shouldered my pack
and, not looking back,
walked out to meet
the infinite grey and the wet fall,
stand by the road thumb out,
pilgrim, supplicant, bum in the rain:
who chooses to leave what he has
must take what he gets.

Why I Write in Coffee Houses and Diners

Saturday Morning, Cafe Du Jour

I think she's sexy—
always half asleep
when she serves my morning coffee,
voice dreamy as she greets me.
There's a quietness in her movements
that draws you toward sleep.
You envision her lying,
limbs scattered,
covers trailing from her
as she drinks sleep ravenously,
every golden inch of her
drawing it in.
Your hands tingle
to the sleep-drenched warmth of her
as she counts out your change
in a blurry voice
and smiles a smile,
shy, mysterious,
intimate with sleep.

Albert Huffstickler

Oracle

The Golden Lady sat down at the table
next to me and ate her popcorn looking off.
I knew she was the Golden Lady.
Blonde and lovely with skin like mist
over a lake at sunrise
and a red halter with white dots.
I think she had a message for me—
something about being young—
but it was hard to decipher
through a mouth full of popcorn.
Perhaps that was the ordeal I must undergo—
deciphering a message about my lost youth
delivered from a mouth full of popcorn.

Why I Write in Coffee Houses and Diners

Not Wounded,
Sire, But Dead

That crazy guy
across the street
talking to the air
isn't so different.
If you put a
cellular phone
in his hand,
he'd be a yuppie.

Albert Huffstickler

Mandate from the Hag

She stood and raged at me
in her rags and wrinkles.
This old crone knew every hole in my armor.
Finally, she put a hand down my throat
and, seizing my heart, yanked,
turned me inside out.
I stood there, vitals exposed,
while her laughter probed me
like tiny scalpels.
"Practice your shame!"
she shrieked in my ear.
"You've failed Humiliation three times!
Do it till you get it right!"
Then she was gone. It was night.
I stood there crying
till the tears filled my inside-our heart
and flowed down the street, a bright,
stricken river touched by starlight.

Why I Write in Coffee Houses and Diners

A Requiem for Mad Helen

Helen, I hear, is dead
who ranged the streets
in costumes and head-
dresses, performing
bizarre, symbolic dances,
climbed trees naked
and dared the cops to
get her down, was
committed and retaliated
by organizing the
patients, only woman
to be evicted from
the state hospital,
the staff having decided
that they needed asylum
more than she did.
Not many could handle
her rage, pain and
ugly bitterness. Today
it rains and the rain
brings ghosts and it
will soon be autumn,
a fitting time for
Helen's ghost to
dance along wet Austin's
streets, mad as a
hatter and with the
hats to prove it.

Albert Huffstickler

God of the forsaken,
alleycats, artists,
mendicants, madmen and bums,
keep her by you
till the resurrection comes.

Why I Write in Coffee Houses and Diners

Cafe Du Jour

She stopped at the entrance,
peered inside
anxious-eyed,
turned,
turned back,
finally came in,
then turned again
and fled.
On the final turn,
I almost spoke,
almost said, "It's O.K."
But didn't.
How could I know
the next step
in that intricate dance?
I couldn't hear the music.
No, I sat on,
a part of the scenery,
and watched her go,
feeling cold suddenly,
separate,
and very much afraid
for all of us.

Albert Huffstickler

Cafe Poem

That little old lady has a purpose.
She's a cartographer completing the map of
 her life.
It's there on her face,
as contained, as exact as the will that lies
deep in that small, shrunken breast.
She looks around her, laughs.
Another line forms,
another move toward the completion she
 already envisions.
There's nothing more for us here.
Let's leave her to her work.

Why I Write in Coffee Houses and Diners

The Search

Juicy Lucy loves Fat Oscar
Graffiti in Men's Room, Les Amis

Which brings us to the subject
of how people find each other.
Does anyone know?
I don't.
I've been looking all my life.
There must be somebody.
Which is why
I read all graffiti carefully.
There may a message for me.
I mean,
if Juicy Lucy found Fat Oscar,
there's still hope,
isn't there?

Albert Huffstickler

Vigil

I keep waiting.
One more cup.
I will hold
this world still
till what I want
appears.
The girl in
the narrow
red dress
walks tethered
from the room
on stiletto heels,
her head
a round black bowl
with golden handles
precariously
balanced on
her thin shoulders.

Why I Write in Coffee Houses and Diners

Augury

That little old lady
across the room
is eating a hotdog on a stick.
She eats slowly,
savoring it.
She has nachos too
and all the time in the world.
It's true:
you can see it in her face.
I feel the earth tilt slightly
and readjust its orbit,
settling around her
while she nibbles on,
smiling to herself.
And me—
I light a cigarette,
lean back and relax,
trusting her,
knowing there's still time.

Albert Huffstickler

Respite

Sylvia across the table from me
at the Tower Restaurant, pregnant,
eating strawberry ice cream (she'd
have eaten it all day and night if
she could, would have mainlined it
if she'd found a way). We'd just
put the laundry in at Ching Wong and
come here on this summer breezy day
in Sixties Austin, Sylvia eating
ice cream and me drinking coffee,
smoking, nothing to do but let the
laundry cook—silent, you don't start
talking till something's wrong and
nothing was wrong for the time being
in Sixties Austin with the sun bearing
down and the light just so and the
laundry in and strawberry ice cream
and coffee and cigarettes and silence
and if you think this poem is going
anywhere, you're mistaken.

Why I Write in Coffee Houses and Diners

Need

There was a pullman diner about a block
from the Canyon Hotel where I lived in
    Flagstaff.
I used to eat Sunday breakfast there,
a special treat after my week washing dishes
at the Branding Iron Cafe. It was very small
and you had to wait in line and then crowd
up to the counter where the stools were too
close together and eat elbow to elbow with
your partners on each side, which would seem
a discomfort unless you'd been living all
summer in a town where you knew no one.
Then it became just live contact and necessary.
The low ceiling compressed odors—bodies and
bacon and coffee—and blended them into a
totally human essence that, transformed by
loneliness, became the most fragrant possible
    perfume.
I lingered over coffee and cigarettes until
the press of the crowd compelled me to leave.
Reluctantly, I rose, walked back outside to
the suddenly gaping streets and walked and
walked, hunched into myself, dreading even
as I relished the freedom of my day—walked
till I was too tired to think or feel anything
then trudged back to my small room to fall
across the bed and drift off to fierce, tormenting
dreams that thrust me back to wakefulness

Albert Huffstickler

and the sudden evening to lie on my bed
watching the night gather outside my window,
feeling it grow, hearing the hum of evening
punctuated by that most despairing of
lamentations, the shrill cry of a drunk Indian.
Sirens roared, a bottle crashed against a wall,
then slowly, ever so slowly, like muted strings,
the rain began.

Why I Write in Coffee Houses and Diners

The Lost Poem

My father carried a poem with
him all through his internment
in Cabanatuan prison camp in
the Philippines, carried it
with him for four years, showed
it to me one day folded and
refolded, print blurred, coming
apart. I, in my teens, not
thinking, nodded and went on
and forgot. Years later, I
tried to recall what poem it
was, even a single line of it,
but it was gone. The years
go by, both he and my mother dead
this long time. There's no one to
ask. So I ponder it. And
ponder motivations, what drives
us, ponder what drives me still
to write with the same intensity
after all these years. And ponder
the lost poem. Perhaps that's
part of it: I'm driven to create
that poem I can't recall, the
poem that carried him through
four years of Hell and home
again. Or perhaps I'm driven
to write a poem that will serve
someone else as well. It's a
nice thought anyway: my poem
in someone's pocket, bent
and faded, nourishing him, healing

Albert Huffstickler

him, through his own private
Hell. A man could do worse
with his life. I evoke my
father's image, our eyes meet,
he nods in agreement, starts
to speak then turns and walks
off into the distance, bearing
the lost poem with him.

Why I Write in Coffee Houses and Diners

The Healing

I dreamed last night of a man with a
wounded mouth and a
wounded heart and the
wounds were the same shape.
I woke thinking of my father,
dead these many years, who
lost his larynx to cancer and learned
how to speak by belching—only he
couldn't speak long sentences so
he had to write things down.
I thought about how his inability to articulate
drove him to writing
just as my own inarticulateness drove me.
And somehow it seemed that our stories were one
and that was the story I had to write. And
it came to me also that
even though a man sees his destiny,
it's still on him to choose it.
The road is there before him but
he still must choose to walk it
as I choose now to walk
this spiraling road down to myself,
this road that is both mine and his,
this road that leads to a place I have yet to find—
where all wounds are healed
and the words come of themselves.

Albert Huffstickler

Ministry

Theo is gone from the Plaza Restaurant in
    Santa Fe
and I wonder what happened to Irene
who worked that coffee shop in Flagstaff.
And Isobel who worked the counter at
    Woolworth's in Santa Fe
and broad-hipped Ruth at the Palms Restaurant
    in Fort Myers
and dark-eyed Chris who fed the transients
at the Rexall lunch counter on Guadalupe Street
    in Austin.
I wonder what happened to them.
I wonder if they ever got back half as much as
    they gave
to the shabby men who crouched at their
    counters
in the cosmic dusk of a lonely planet.

Why I Write in Coffee Houses and Diners

Echoes

Mario Lanza kept me going for a year once.
I as working at the Snack House in Fort Myers,
clearing tables, split shift—lunch and supper
with three hours off in between, a draining
and uninspiring job. Sometimes I didn't even
go home in between, just walked across the street
to Kinander's Record Store and drenched myself
in that gorgeous voice then, saturated with
melody and longing, crossed back over for
another five hours of clearing tables.
I was young then. It didn't take too much.
I dreamed my way from table to table and,
before you knew it, my shift was over.
Later, I went on to other things and Mario Lanza
ate and drank himself to death and that
glorious voice went down to the dust.
But the memory endures.
I wouldn't take anything for it.
Time eats us bones and all but some memories
are beyond its reach. That's the only way
we know that, try though it may,
it won't get all of us.

Albert Huffstickler

Dream Come True

I remember sitting in a drugstore at 19
in Ft. Myers, Florida, drinking coffee
(with my last nickel probably) and
smoking when I was supposed to be
looking for a job, watching the people,
daydreaming, thinking how it would be
to have nothing to do but go from
place to place drinking coffee, smoking,
watching the people and writing with
no pressure on you, no job to look
for—or go to, nothing but just that:
watching people and writing, not having
to force your head in any direction it
didn't want to go, not having to think
about things you didn't want to think
about, not having to force yourself
to focus, not having to break you
heart against a world that you had
no understanding of, no real feeling
for, no talent for. Now suddenly
fifty years have passed and, as if by
magic, my dream has come true. I
really don't have anything to do but
wander around, sit in restaurants and
cafes and write when I feel like it.
That's it. They call it retirement—
the only occupation I was ever really
suited for. And you want to know
something? It's every bit as good
as I thought it would be.

Why I Write in Coffee Houses and Diners

Key West

In Key West
they serve Espresso
in the Cuban restaurants
and it's very hot and sticky
and black, presweetened,
served in tiny juice glasses,
slender, with just about an inch in
the bottom and you sip it
slowly, small sips till it's
diffused through your mouth,
stomach and from there, sweet
and vibrant, through every inch
of your flesh till all of you
is warm and fragrant, steeped.
It costs a nickel
and makes the morning.
Where else can you find
a bargain like that?

Albert Huffstickler

Markings

Joanna Nelson was here.
Aug. 18, 1985

This is to certify
that Joanna Nelson
waited for the bus
at the Highland Mall bus stop
and saw fit to declare it
to all and sundry
with a felt tip pen
on the wall of the shelter,
declaring a fact
while creating a mystery
as women are so often
prone to do.
It won't last.
Felt tip ink weathers
an fades, smears too.
You can hardly read the date.
In a month it will be gone.
No record will remain
of Joanna Nelson's sojourn
at the Highland Mall bus stop
and we'll be the less for it.
We need to know that.
We need to remember
before all our personal records
are washed away
in a tide of computer printouts.
We need to find Joanna Nelson

Why I Write in Coffee Houses and Diners

before it's too late.
We need to find out
who she is and what she did
at the Highland Mall bus stop
on Aug. 18, 1995.
We need to do it *now*.
It just may be
the most important thing in the world.
Where are you, Joanna Nelson?
We need to see your face.

Albert Huffstickler

Queen of the Royal Castle

Taking a little old lady almost eighty,
dizzy from high blood pressure,
to the Royal Castle for a hamburger isn't a
    poem—
even though she prefers this place above all others,
even though she sits very primly with her eyes
    shining,
sipping her coke and munching her dollar-size
    burger,
thin as a communion wafer,
even though this is the very heart of life to her,
riding very straight on the seat beside you,
smelling of talcum, head poised like a bird's,
    luxuriating:
out of the house,
out of the cage of TV and loneliness,
free in the sun with a strong son beside her.
This couldn't be poetry—
even though it took her two hours to get ready,
prissing and bustling and murmuring to herself,
"At last! At last The Royal Castle!"—
even though the trip would cost her
a day in bed and perhaps another week
of listing from room to room barely keeping her
    balance.
Poetry? No.
Just something to remember
when you feel like rolling your life up
like a wad of old gum
and sticking it under the table.

Why I Write in Coffee Houses and Diners

Found

She found me on the bench
in front of the Hyde Park Bakery,
middle-aged baglady or
stray from the State Hospital.
"You rich?" she asked.
"Got enough to buy me a soda water?
I got three cents.
I just came from borrowing a bathroom."
I figured anybody
that had to borrow a bathroom
deserved the price of a soda water
so I gave her fifty cents
and she sat on a while
smoking a cigarette,
filling my space with her space
till we both had enough space
to last a lifetime.
Then she gathered her bundles
and went off down the street
moving with the same slow solemn gait
that fate moves
entering or leaving our lives.

Albert Huffstickler

Criminal Intent

That guy who spent the night
on the bench in front of the bakery
was rousted by the cops.
I guess they got him for
Sleeping Without A License.
That's right up there with
Breathing With Intent To Live.

Why I Write in Coffee Houses and Diners

A Blessing Poem

The peace of loneliness be with you
The peace of the far-from-home
The peace of small things intricately woven
like those moments in time that come
out of nowhere small and bright and eternal
The peace of loneliness be with you
and the patience of the stranger
who would not be known too soon
The peace of warm fires and sudden silences
and small gifts willingly given
and the peace of birds across a strange sky
singing in the early morning
and the peace of lakes and hidden ponds
and small streams silvering a hidden meadow
The peace of those who walk alone
knowing that in the heart of loneliness
their true home is hidden
waiting for that moment of silence and truth
in which to reveal itself
The peace of loneliness be with you
The peace of corner booths in coffee shops
by highways a thousand miles from home
The peace of old fabric and ancient wood
and the peace of stone which knows only itself

Albert Huffstickler

The peace of churches and silent houses
and the peace of grass newly mown
The peace of loneliness be with you
The peace of starlight on a distant road
The peace of trees and small animals beneath
    the ground
The peace of all creatures far from home
The peace of loneliness be with you
for in your loneliness you are not alone.

About the Author

Albert Huffstickler is a poet and artist whose work has appeared internationally in small and literary publications since the early 1970s. The Texas State Senate passed a resolution honoring him in 1989; and in 1997, he was honored at the International Poetry Festival in Austin, Texas, where he lives and writes. Huffstickler's *Walking Wounded*, which chronicles his stay at a convalescence home following surgery, won the Austin Book Award in 1989 and was published by Backyard Press. *Working on My Death Chant*, supported by a grant from the City of Austin, Texas, under the auspices of the Austin Arts Commission and the Texas Commission for the Arts, was published by Backyard Press in 1991, and Sulphur River Literary Review Press published *The Wander Years* in 1998. A number of chapbooks under his own imprint, Press of Circumstance, have been produced in the past twenty years. These publications include *City of the Rain*, a memorial to Flagstaff, Arizona, and a granddaughter. Huffstickler's poems have been anthologized in a number of collections, including *Grow Old Along with Me, The Best is Yet to Be*, edited by Sandra Martz (Papier Mache Press, 1996) and *I Feel a Little Jumpy Around You: A Book of Her Poems and His Poems* by Naomi Shihab Nye and Paul B. Janeczko (Simon & Schuster, 1996). Glosso Babel set "Huff's Funk (Newsreel '75)" to music for *Babble Lingus* (1997).

The son of a career soldier and a schoolteacher, Huffstickler was born in Laredo, Texas, December 17, 1927, and grew up on army bases around the country. He lived in Kings Mountain, North Carolina, during his teens and attended the University of North Carolina at Chapel Hill before serving in the army. He later graduated from San Marcos State University in Texas. Huffstickler's career includes a variety of jobs across the country, particularly in Florida, New Mexico, Arizona, and Texas. For a number of years until his

Why I Write in Coffee Houses and Diners

retirement, he worked for General Libraries of The University of Texas at Austin. Huffstickler has been active in the poetry scene in Austin since the 1960s. Currently he serves as poetry editor of *Pecan Press*, a publication of the Hyde Park Neighborhood Association, and makes his home in Austin.